CRESCENT BANK & TRUST

CORPORATE CRIME OVER INDIVIDUALS IN AMERICAN JUSTICE SYSTEM THROUGH AUTO LOANS.

The legal trick of Homan Mobasser: CA. Bar No. 251426

Emmanuel Adetula

Emmanuel Adetula

This book was printed in United States May, 2014

To order additional copies of this book:

Write to:

Emmanuel Adetula

Mailing: P.O. BOX 1017 Lawndale, CA.90260

E-mail: tulatax@gmail.com

Website: www.christchannelnetwork.org

ABOUT THIS BOOK

Every year, the major business magazines put out their annual surveys of big business in America. You have the Fortune 500, the Forbes 400, and the Forbes Platinum 100 among others. The point of these magazines surveys is simple -- to identify and glorify the biggest and most profitable corporations. But nobody put out annual surveys to reveal the dark underside of the marketplace that is given little sustained attention and analysis by politicians and news outlets. In this book I am publishing a story in regard to Case number 12CT3326 at the SUPERIOR COURT OF CALIFORNIA, COUNTY OF LOS ANGELES to reveal to the general public how CRESCENT BANK & TRUST top the list of Corporate Criminals in America in 2014 and how PROBER & RAPHAEL , A LAW CORPORATION who based his office at 20750 Ventura Blvd. Suite 100 Woodland Hills , CA. 91364 top the list of worst legal firms in America in 2014. This Law firm is using the Los Angeles County Judicial System to perpetuate the likes of Crescent Bank & Trust corporate crime on hundreds of innocent Citizens in California, This law firm continues to take advantage of immigrants ignorance and thousands of Americans using the Los Angeles Superior Court process to make profits for this Bank and their own legal firm, and these Attorneys at PROBER & RAPHAEL continue to use their legal tricks to manipulate some departments of the Los Angeles County to make this corporate crime works for the banks, and the Los Angeles Superior Court Judges and the County of Los Angeles Register – Recorder/County Clerk office are now locked in the legal box of this Corporate crime that favors corporate crime over Individuals minority poor people in America.

What is going on California now is that there is an emerging consensus among corporate criminologists that the Los Angeles County judicial system allows corporate crime to inflicts far more damage on California society than all street crime combined, the way the courts handles and decide on cases as enumerated in this book should be look at from The FBI estimates, for example, that burglary and robbery -- street crimes -- costs the nation $3.8 billion a year. Compare this to the hundreds of billions of dollars stolen from American Citizens as a result of corporate and white-collar judicial fraud against individuals through American judicial system like Los Angeles Superior Courts as evidenced in this case number 12CT3326 , CRESCENT BANK & TRUST VS EMMANUEL ADETULA

So, in "Crime in the United States" you will read about burglary, robbery and theft. There is nothing in it about an Attorney like Homan Mobasser using legal trick to fix cases that makes banks like Crescent Bank & Trust to commit corporate fraud against Americans, getting a bad court judgment with enforcement by the County of Los Angeles Register –Recorder/County Clerk office.

In this book I did try to assess and compare the damage committed by this corporate criminal by publishing 60 letters from others auto loan customers of Crescent Bank & Trust and this Attorney on records to proof that my own defense presented to court in case #12CT3326 represent the views of millions of Americans who care about morality in the marketplace and how the judicial system in California is being use by the Law firm of PROBER & RAPHAEL to push the courts to favors corporate crimes , Some of these government officials seem to be profiting from this system that effectively has become legalized bribery giving judgment freely to Plaintiff corporation because of bank immense political power, Crescent Bank & Trust as a corporation have the resources to defend itself in courts of law but this my book is for the court of public opinion. The Judges that handled this case #12CT3326 willing allowed themselves to be subjected to the constant legal and public relations barrage that Crescent

Bank & Trust corporation's well connected and high-priced Attorneys of PROBER & RAPHAEL Law Firm represented in this case, as presented to the court by Attorney Homan Mobasser legal trick infliction. This case is not about Homan Mobasser legal professionalism , He is not Smart than me Emmanuel Adetula, He is just a legal trickster, He cannot win me in the court of commonsense argument and the court of public opinion, he is just licensed to play legal trick to enrich corporation and his law firm, this is a Lawyer who play tricks to win in courts , this case was not won on legal grounds but by tricks allowed by Los Angeles County judicial process , taking advantage on poor Americans on Auto Car loans , this same law firm files an average of 100 cases daily to harassed and terrorized innocent Americans who have no money to hire an Attorney for cases that emanated from indirect extortion by Crescent Bank & Trust through PROBER & RAPHEL Law Firm . This is how Los Angeles County Judicial system works whenever they decided a case between a corporation and an individual American, which makes this County judicial system worst than most third world countries. There is nowhere in the world except in America where the justice system is set up to make it so easy for a trickster attorney to manipulate the court to favors corporate criminal like Crescent Bank and Trust.

Emmanuel Adetula

Emmanuel Adetula is an Author of 27 other books.

Get your copy today direct at www.amazon.com

For questions about this book or to request a free copy:-

Write Emmanuel Adetula

tulatax@gmail.com

P.O. BOX 1017

Lawndale, CA. 90260 USA

www.christchannelnetwork.org

CONTENTS

Searching for the truth is the most honorable ministry in this world and it's my most dangerous assignment, after you know the truth, it takes courage to make it known to the public, and making it known to the public may not make you rich, but it will for sure through persecution hatred and glass ceiling over your career force you to reach for God until you become like one of the gods, then What is truth?. Truth is a repeated experiences of life on something that keeps happening to you over and over again, that you have come to know for yourself that whatever may be the thinking, reasoning and arguments of others will no longer alter your opinion and believe about such a thing, because you have come to know from your own personal experiences that this is how this thing works here. I did not get my own truth through religion, tradition, heritage, philosophy, denominational association or through political affiliations, but this is what I know from my own personal experiences with Los Angeles Judicial System, that it favors corporate crime over individuals in America, it takes property from the poor to give to the rich , it sent people to jail for offence they did not commit , it destroy people credit and reputation just because they do not have the money to hire an American judicial system still operates within the parameter of economic slavery, because it favors the rich over the poor. That is the truth told in this book, and what I wrote in this book is supported by 58 other Americans whose own experiences with Crescent Bank is also recorded in this book.

Emmanuel Adetula

ABOUT THE AUTHOR

Dr. Emmanuel Adetula, Master of Arts in Divinity, Doctor of Philosophy in Social Work, Professional Trainings in Philanthropy, Conflict Analysis, Conflict Resolution, Mediation, Negotiation and Conflict Management from The Academy for Conflict and Peace building United States Institute of Peace Academy. Washington, DC. , La Sierra University School of Business, Riverside, California and Pepperdine University School of Law at the Straus Institute for Dispute Resolution. Malibu, California. Member Association of Business Executives, Member Association of Conflict Resolution, Member California Lawyers for the Arts.

Emmanuel Adetula licensed in the state of California USA as a Realtor, CPA/IRS Tax Professional and Notary Public. Current Managing Partner at Emmanuel Tula Associates, Emmanuel Tula Tax Service and Here & There on Time Transports. A Naturalized Citizen of United States, Born in Owo , Ondo State of Nigeria . Primary home at Ibadan, Oyo State Nigeria with Permanent Home at Los Angeles, California - United States of America.

Website: www.emmanueltula.com

Emmanuel Adetula is the Founding President/CEO of Christ Channel Network, bona-fide 501 c 3 nonprofit organizations in United States since 2002, doing business as CCN House Community Development agency, providing housing to homeless individuals and families in USA and CCN Orphan and Vulnerable Children Center. Website: www.christchannelnetwork.org

He is also the President CCN CENTER FOR PEACE. Emmanuel Adetula is an Author of 26 other books, available at online bookstores in paperback and in kindle editions around the world.

JUDGE...WANNA DANCE?
$
INFLUENCE
COMMERCE
ATTORNEYS
$
INFLUENCE

"A nation of sheep will soon have a government of wolves."
- Edward R. Murrow

Crescent Bank & Trust developed relationships with numerous new and used car dealerships across the country in United States whereby Crescent Bank purchases vehicle loans directly from the dealerships and Used Auto Auctions yards. Crescent has focused its auto loan business on sub-prime customers who are often not able to obtain financing through traditional channels. Crescent Bank routinely ignores the actual terms of its customer loan agreements - which are purchased from dozens of different car dealerships across several states - and instead imposes a one-size-fits-all billing and payment system. This practice results in customers paying higher fees, interest, and penalties than authorized by their loan agreements. This company is the worst ever to deal with. Crescent Bank & Trust assessment of Improper Charges in Conjunction with Automobile Loans. This book documents letters received from 58 auto loan consumers whose credit life and reputation have been rip off by Crescent Bank & Trust with the help of Attorneys like PROBER & RAPHAEL, A LAW CORPORATION who based his office at 20750 Ventura Blvd. Suite 100 Woodland Hills, CA. 91364. Crescent Bank is a sub-primary lending financial institution that does what they want to do when they want to do it to capitalize their dollars. All of the members of senior management are racist, they don't speak and they don't take responsibility for wrongful doings that's caused by the company, but quick to fire you if they find something wrong that you've done. They are over-charging consumers in interest, late fees and penalties and have a law firm like Prober & Raphael behind them using the Los Angeles Superior Court Judges to perpetuate their corporate crime against minorities and the poor people of America.

Crescent Bank are reporting incorrect information about car loan consumers account to all the credit agencies without mention of the facts surrounding these car loans and good faith payments in the past , the intentional and malicious damage done by this bank has caused untold hardships of unemployment to thousands of families in America, even the government of United States denied employment to this bank victims just because of Crescent Bank & Trust consumers reports to credit agencies, on this same Crescent Bank & Trust , its auto loan customers received Court debtor judgments at the courts leading to public lien on their primary home for auto loan at Los Angeles County-Recorders office which becomes bad public records , and this public records and credits reports that came from false reports created by the corporate crime of Crescent Bank & Trust and its Debt collectors Attorney office of PROBER & RAPHAEL is being used to create unemployment and make life difficult financially for the minorities in America by this racist Bank and Legal firm.

Crescent Bank is based out of LA. However, it has a sister company in Virginia named Crescent Recovery that 90% of the company work Crescent Bank & Trust loans as of 1/1/13. Crescent Recovery is no longer in existence after they destroyed thousands of Americans credit records, they now merged with Crescent Bank & Trust and I'm quite sure it was because Crescent Recovery could no longer handle the lawsuits she was being faced with by consumers , but California courts is still respecting this company who has been rejected by other states as corporate criminal, and smart enough employees that stand up against this company in the past can tell you how far PROBER & RAPHAEL Law firm are using the California judicial system to smile to the bank through this corporate crime. On too many occasions, this company has not paid the employees' bonus because of a software/system problem or because not one person is on the same page as others, the managers don't know what the collection department is doing.

When you become an assistant collections manager, you're not trained properly; they stick you out there to teach yourself or to just flat out learn from your mistakes. How fair is this to the regular employees that are actually calling the customers, collecting the payments, and negotiating with consumers on how to remedy their financial problems? This company has the ability of moving accounts around as they please but will not take responsibility of their multi-million dollar system that no one knows how to operate "Our systems are down, your rep will have to call you and follow-up on your concern when the system is back up and running."

The only thing this company is designed to do is get over! It was also designed for the bank to gain more interest off the customers. Customers receive late fees that they shouldn't be receiving. An example is a customer has been outside of the grace period 4 times and has been assessed $67.00 in late charges. If the customer gets back on track with monthly payments without paying late fees, the next on time payment, Crescent will take the $67.00, apply it to the fees which leaves the customer's car payment $67.00 short.

Accounts are not reviewed until after they have come out the grace period which is 11 days for most accounts; that means the customer has gained 11 days of interest on top of that, another late fee. Then CB&T, if they catch the error, has to submit a reverse/reapply form to a supervisor. That sits an additional 2 days before the posting department fixes the error. That means that this bank has gained 13-14 days of additional money. They do not refund any of this money back to the customer and stays rich. It's up to the representative to waive the new late fee if not, that increases the late fee balance and this same thing will happen again, and again, and again each month until the customer included the additional money to cover the fees. This is illegal! They had an "investigation case" on some employees that were entering fake/false checks on customers' accounts so they could hit goal.

The case must be still under investigation because the same people are still employed with the company. As a matter of fact, the main person behind the scandal got promoted to collections manager, ha! Granted she was black, there was no investigation and the account got shuffled around to other reps' queues to band aid the wrongful doing. Most recent, they suspended a supervisor with no pay (she was also a part of the entering in fake/false check scandal) for reversing and reapplying a payment that was misapplied (a legit reversal) by the bank because the account remained delinquent and it should've been current, but the misapplied payment was caught several months later. Who cares when you catch it as long as it's caught so our customers are treated fairly? No, the bank wants to keep the money because the more accounts that are reversed and reapplied, the more money is deducted from the bank profits.

How can a customer that makes a car payment with no special instructions to apply to anything else be at fault? If these bank customers pay as early as a day before the due date, the funds are going to be applied to late fees/miscellaneous fees until further investigations. This is the smallest bank you could ever work for to have so many members of senior management yet still has no organization. You could walk in this office, ask 10 people 1 question and you'll get 10 different answers. This bank is bad and they need to be shut down and their Attorney office in Los Angeles PROBER & RAPHAEL Law firm should be investigated alongside cases handled by them representing this bank through the Los Angeles Superior Court System like in case #12CT3326

Read the following letters to the general public from Americans who have been rip off by Crescent Bank and its racist Attorneys.

1. We had purchased a vehicle with a high interest loan. (23.9%) Our loan was originally with American Investment Bank and sold several times till we ended up with Crescent. We fell behind and wanted to sell the car. We had serious buyers and could have gotten 3,000.00 + for the vehicle. They couldn't wait one extra day. Told them where to pick up car & keys, etc. They repo'd car and sold at auction for a little over $1,000.00.

   Balance owed was still $4,000.00. I sold my house and tried to negotiate with them. We agreed over phone to $1700.00. They faxed over agreement to the tune of $2,500.00. I called right back and they said that was interest. (In hindsight I should have agreed to that amount). I refused to sign and they eventually turned me over to a lawyer. They sent a summons stating we needed to contact them within 10 days or be sued.

   I again contacted their legal team and tried to work out a repayment plan. They wanted me to still pay interest up until I signed. I did not like the wording of the agreement and was also advised by an atty. not to sign their agreement. Go to court and the judge would most likely throw out all the interest. (Which is what I wanted)? Well a year later I received a judgment to garnish wages with no notice that they had indeed filed charges.

I am now owing $8000.00. What a rip off this company is. I am trying to reopen the case to be heard by a judge. I am praying that we will at least have our day in court. They have been charging 23.9% on a car neither one of us still has. We know we owe the principal but we purchased the car when it was 4 years old and more than paid for what it sold for brand new.

Linda
Henderson, Nevada
U.S.A.

2. Have had a loan with them since 2/05, car was financed for four years.
   FIRST ISSUE: A couple of weeks after purchasing car, receive letter stating that I need to provide them with proof of insurance or they will charge me for insurance using their own insurance company or take the car. I gave them proof of insurance twice, on the day that I purchased the vehicle and my insurance company mailed them proof to the address that they told me to send it to.

   SECOND ISSUE: Review my payment book and find that even though I have a set monthly payment for what is supposed to be the life of my loan (four years), the final payment coupon states that the buyer must contact them for the amount of the final payment. HUH?? Why??? I have bought and paid for at least 6 cars in my lifetime and this is the FIRST time I have EVER seen this in a payment book.

After reading some of the issues that others have stated regarding loan amounts changing and loans being extended without their permission, I now can see how Crescent may be setting up buyers for deceptive lending practices.

THIRD ISSUE: They do NOT send you statements so that you can see what your account activity looks like and if you request one you will NEVER receive one. I never have.

FOURTH ISSUE: It is not possible to get a payoff amount. I have tried, when I was considering trading in the car, I tried and could not get it.

I used to mail my payments into these people, but after receiving their asinine phone calls a couple of days before my payment was due asking me when I was sending in my payment (remember now--it is NOT even due yet and I am getting phone calls), I started to just use Western Union. It provides a very clear record of payment sent, payment received. I highly suggest that if you are a victim/customer of this bank that you send payments via Western Union or Moneygram. If you speak with them about anything, record your phone conversations or handle all communication in writing with signature receipt confirmation. If you make payments by check, send it by certified check or use an online bill payment service that will electronically record payments for you.

Arguing with these people is useless; the only manner of communication they understand is the sign language--the dollar sign. If you have legal issues with them, contact an attorney and let the attorney handle ALL communication with them.

If you get behind on a payment, include ANY and ALL late charges with ALL payments. Indicate on the payment what the actual payment amount is and what the late charge is. In fact, if you can, make these payments individually. Send on payment for the payment and another for any late fees--with the description annotated on the payments.

If you enter into any type of modified payment agreement with these people, get it in writing and/or record the conversation or have a legal representative present during the negotiations.

My loan is due to end in a few months and I am already

anticipating that I will have issues getting the car title. It just seems like their mode of operation.

Saraha
Houston, Texas
U.S.A.

3. My fiancée had her loan account with other bank companies before it went to Crescent Bank & Trust, she had her car for about 2 years and the last 4 or 5 months it was with Crescent Bank & Trust. My fiancée was 2 month pass due in her loan payment and they never told her that she was pass due or ever sent her notice of her balances. My fiancée never told me that she was pass due until the day before they had repo her car because she is a strong woman and don't like help from anybody, not even me. My fiancée try her best to keep up with her payments but with the way gas and food is going up every day it was real hard for her.
My fiancée finally came to me for support and help but before I could help her the repos was at her door to take her only transportation and then she call me to come over. When I got to her house I talk to the men that was there and told them I was willing to pay the past due amount which was $700 but the repo men said it was not $700 past due it was $3500 past due. As my fiancée and I look at the amount that was given to the repo men she burst out and cried, she told the men that were not the right amount and that she was only 2 months pass due. The repo men told her if that's true then aren't no way they

would have been sent to repo a car that is only 2 months pass due. The repo men also said that it seems like somebody at Crescent Bank & Trust lied and made a false pass due amount just to get the car repo.

My fiancée showed me her all the payments she made on the car and to everybody who is reading this she was right, she was only 2 months pass due. We tried calling and got know answer then I got in contact with a man who the head of the accounting department and he is Mr. Williams and he did not have any information on the my fiancée account and Mr. Williams stated that he did not have anything showing on his computer screen that the car was repo or anything showing the car was suppose to get repo and he suppose to be the head person who handle the repo case(yea right) it sounds like some people in Mr. Williams department is doing whatever they want to do and there is no rules there. Crescent bank & Trust did not care that people are struggling for food and gas, Crescent Bank & Trust did not care that my fiancée made her payments on time or ahead the past year; Crescent Bank & Trust don't care that my fiancée might have to quite her job because there is not any buses where she live. If Crescent Bank & Trust was a good bank they would have work with us or try to give her time to get her account up to date that's what good business companies do to their great customers because every customers is a good customer but Crescent Bank & Trust do not do that because they hustle people and they lie. Crescent Bank & Trust do not care about people that are affected with food and gas prices going up and the way

they are treating people it seems like they are kicking people while they are down and my fiancée told me that's how she feels. How are we going to pay a amount that they made up and get the car back well I tell you what they don't want us to get it back because they are going to give it to somebody else to f*ck over accuse my French, all they are doing is hustling people and that the honest god truth. I would not stop and I will keep fighting no matter what happens.
Please if anybody gets the number to the president of Crescent Bank & Trust please posted up on this web page so I can start calling him or her every day all day trust me I will because starting tomorrow I will be calling Mr. Williams every day all day until we come to agreement. They should not have made my fiancée cry. they hustled the wrong From Todd of Centennial, CO on July 21, 2010

We had purchased a '93 Mercury Mountaineer. Our loan was with Crescent Bank and Trust out of New Orleans La. We always sent our payment on time via mail. The bank does not dispute that but they had our car repossessed anyway. On account of the Katrina hurricane damage, our payment was late. They demanded we pay them balance owed and tow charges totaling several thousand dollars. We could not afford that so they sold the car and continued to charge us interest. They sent the loan to Crescent recovery and put it on our credit profiles all the while charging interest on a loan of $4,192.21. The result was the devastation of our credit.

4. I had an automobile loan that was turned over to Crescent Bank and Trust for collection. After the car was auctioned off I was told I was responsible for the remaining balance. I gave my wife, Amanda Tuttle, permission to handle all business associated with the account. She came to an agreement with a representative of Crescent Bank and Trust to pay $25.00 a month.

   The representative called every week even though we were sending our payments. Finally she told us that $25.00 a month was not enough and she couldn't accept payments that low anymore. My wife explained to her that we were limited in income and $25.00 was all we could afford. The representative claimed that was not enough and she couldn't accept that amount. She got very rude wanting to know why I couldn't take a second job to make higher payments, why my wife couldn't get a job to make the payments, why couldn't we let another bill go to make higher payments, etc. My wife finally told her that since she couldn't accept our money as per our agreement anymore then our responsibility for this debt was finished.

   We made an agreement and honored it up until we were told our money would no longer be accepted. Because our money was refused we are no longer liable for this debt. It is still collecting interest and Crescent Bank and Trust is still calling repeatedly. We have told them to stop calling us because we are no longer responsible for this debt. They have harassed us to the point of intolerance and they have reported incorrect information about this account to all the credit agencies without mention of the fact that we did not make good faith payments nor the fact that we were told our money would no longer be accepted.

They have submitted conflicting information to the different credit reporting agencies. There has been no activity on this account in quite some time yet they are reporting recent activity.

James
Louisville, Kentucky
U.S.A.

5. I became disabled after financing my car through Crescent Bank & Trust, and called to ask if I could change my payment due date as I now receive a benefit check on the first of the month, and the payment is due at the end of the month. I explained I did not wish to be late every month, and this would alleviate that problem.

   I was told this should not be any problem, and a customer service representative faxed me an application to request a date change. I returned the fax, and was later told they could not change the date, because "this would alter the terms of the loan, and put the payment schedule off".

   I pointed out the fact that they would be receiving their payment EARLIER, not later in the month. I was then late on a payment after this request was denied, and this would not have happened had they worked with me.

   I received a call about a late payment from a Crescent

employee, who said she could not understand why they would not work with me. She tried to ask her supervisor, and was denied. She seemed confused, because she stated they routinely granted these requests. I now have to pay a late fee of $15.00 EVERY MONTH. They are clearly doing this to make more money off of my misfortune. At an 18% interest rate, they are getting rich anyway.

I now have to endure a call from this woman every month, even though I have never failed to make any payments, and in keeping with the other reports I see here, I have been threatened with repossession if a payment is not made THAT DAY. She seems genuinely sympathetic and apologizes, but can't seem to get her company to budge. We are now on a first name basis and simply leave voice mails about the fact my payment is coming, just to cover her from being disciplined.

Of course, upon asking for a lower interest rate, it was denied, because I'm "high risk". Gee, I can pay the obscenely high rate every month, but cannot be trusted to pay a lower rate...Avoid them at all costs, Predatory Lender!!!

Mark
Kettering, Ohio
U.S.A.

6. I am writing this report because, as many others, I feel that I have been treated unfairly. In many of the reports that I read against Crescent Bank I found situations similar to mine and it is unfortunate that a company that seems to be growing at such a fast rate, would have so many complaints against them already. I did some research and this company was just established in 1991. As others, my loan was sold 3 different times before ending up at Sylvia's desk at Crescent Bank.

   This is the most unpleasant "customer service rep" I have ever had in my entire life. I have also talked with her supposed "supervisor" who did not even have accurate account information regarding my loan. They are so unpleasant that I decided to see if I could sign up for online payment so that the money would be taken out of my account automatically. I did not have their web site so I searched for Crescent Bank and ended up here instead!

   My vehicle has not been repossessed but I feel that I run the risk of them coming to take my car any minute. As of right now I am not even 30 days late. I receive harassing phone calls at work from my "customer service rep" stating that if I do not pay my car note via western union by the end of the business day, they will repossess my vehicle. I have had my vehicle for almost 5 years and I have every intention to make my final 4 payments on this vehicle. In the 5 years that I have had this car, I have been late several times. At one point I was up to 90 days late and had never been treated the way this company does business. It is absolutely ridiculous. After reading these reports it has opened my eyes. I understand that I am not being singled out and misled alone. We need to come together and stand against companies like these. This type of treatment should be looked at very closely. I hope that my report helps someone who is in my situation.

Mary
Locust Grove, Georgia
U.S.A.

7. Ever since I started paying payments on my car I noticed the principal amount never seems to be lowered. I'm wondering what the hell type of people is running this business and who gave them a certified business license in the first place. It makes no sense how this has been going on for X amount of years and nothing still has been done to this day. I have the same problem as everyone else, if a bill is late they charge a late fee which ok is fine, however, the bill that has incurred the late fee is less than my normal monthly bill. Now tell me how the *#@% that is possible. That makes no sense.

I think this company needs to be put out of business and people should be refunded the money that is due to them. I also believe that our credit should not be tampered with in accordance to their mistakes. This is by far a terrible feeling when you cannot even trust a bank, what is this world coming to.

Jose
Manassas, Virginia
U.S.A.

8. I was late on payments, made arrangements to pay, paid payments never applied to account, interest accumulated, tried at least 10 times to get account cleared up, no one wanted to listen, would not accept copies of payments from my bank, never notified of repossessing vehicle, then was told I couldn't get my personal belongings and plates from vehicle,

   explained police said I could then had to pay $35 charge to get them, received letter I could get vehicle back for 2 payments which I wasn't behind and a fee of $400+, called again to speak with collection manager and tried to go over account and was told she would return my call that she didn't have time to discuss, to this date no call. Very rude people working at this bank, I believe the records should be checked as repo man told me that most of his business now is with crescent bank.

Janeene
Purling, New York
U.S.A.

9. I bought a car from bohn ford in April of 2003 my interest rate was 33% but I needed a vehicle. I bought 1500 dollars worth of warranty when I got financed. Until this day bohn ford has not honored my warranty, but CRESCENT bank and their affiliates are crooks. My payment book was never received. I don't know when my note is due. My note is 311.00 on a 98 ford Windstar.

Recently I got a letter stating my car would be repoed but before that I got a call from a guy claiming to be the president of the bank. His attitude was so unprofessional. His tone was supposed to intimidate me "he said we have problems with you and if you don’t call me we will blah blah blah." I called and I couldn't reach this guy, so I made the payments. A month or so later, they came to get the car from my mother's and I wasn’t there.

I got a letter at my mother's saying to call, so I did. When I talked to Ms. Woodard on the phone she said I was three payments behind. This was on a Wednesday. I said you rather have your money than to have a car back. I told them I can make the payment on that Friday (note that I'm on a new job that they haven't called yet). They got me fired off my last one for calling like we have kids together.

Ms. Woodard put me thru to her supervisor. I said I can make this payment in full Friday, in full. She told me NO and that she needed $940.oo today or it was going to be repoed. Then she added "don't think the repo man don't work on thanksgiving. He will be there to get it. Oh and give him a plate for me. Happy holidays she hung up laughing." they just don't know what kind of a problem they got on their hands now.

Gerard
new Orleans, Louisiana
U.S.A.

10. This company has called my job and family members explaining that I was late only 30 days. Asked if my family members, could they help me get caught up. I had requested that the car be picked up several times and no has attempted to come and get the car yet. I no longer want to be involved or deal with a company that call and give out personal information. this should be against the law for them to do such things.

Outraged
Columbia, South Carolina
U.S.A.

11. Initially, my car loan was through Pinnacle Financial in the month of March 2008. In June of 2008, I received a letter from Crescent Bank & Trust stating that they took over my automobile loan. I fell on financial hardship and the representatives from Crescent Bank & Trust were very nice, and they worked with me. However, beginning in February 2009, I began receiving telephone calls from a Dominquez **, and the calls were continuous with threats of repossession if I did not submit a payment right away because I was behind.

I was appalled and asked to speak with her manager, Kevin **. On two separate occasions, both parties hung up the telephone on me. Mr. ** even stated that, "You won't get no rest" as a means to coerce a payment out of me. I wrote a letter to the President and CEO of Crescent Bank & Trust, Mr. Fred Morgan, along with the Vice President, informing them of the appalling behavior by their staff and I did not receive a verbal or written response from either of them pertaining to the issue.

I did the best to my ability to catch up, and then I got laid off by my job in March of 2008. I informed Ms. ** that I lost my job, however the continuous phone calls came in 3-5 times a week, on a weekly basis threatening to repossess my vehicle if I did not make an immediate payment. In

May of 2008, I did an extension agreement, and within my exchange through the Better Business Bureau, with Ms. Marie **, the Paralegal for Crescent Bank & Trust. Ms. ** acknowledged that my next payment would be due on June 21, 2009. However, I still received phone calls every day, Monday - Friday from Ms. **'s office. I did not understand why I was still being harassed if my payment was due on June 21st. However, due to my finances, I was unable to make that payment on June 21st, but in July I made the payment for June 21st.

Three days after my checked had been cashed, I received a telephone call from a repossession company and they informed me that they had received a vehicle repossession order for my vehicle. I was confused as to why the order would have been issued because I had just made the payment for June. I was told that they would check into it. At approximately 10:00 that evening, a tow truck came to repossess my vehicle, and the following day, I was told that I was 30 days behind on my payment. I am now without a vehicle that should have never been repossessed in the first place, and I have suffered emotionally due to the harassing telephone calls along with the loss of my vehicle. I wish for this to be resolved, and my vehicle released back to me.

12. We have had our loan for just over 1 year and never been 30 days late. We have been a few days late a couple of times due to the dates that my checks fall on and have received calls from them before and after the due dates along with family members. Constantly getting calls from them even when we are not 1 day late. I have tried to speak to several reps about our account and consistently get yelled at and been cursed at more than once. We have always paid more than the monthly payment and after looking at my credit report, it shows I still owe the same amount as what we started out the loan with. I asked how this is possible after making monthly payments + extra and was told it's all interest and that the additional was not going towards the principal. So my $300+ monthly payments are just interest and at this rate I will never pay off the loan. . Alicia of Newnan, GA on March 15, 2014

13. I got the 2008 Chevy Aveo from a car dealership in my town, a few months later the loan was sold to Crescent Bank & Trust (who by the way is still reporting the car loan as IIB). I have made my payments on time for the last two years and they will not work with me. I have two extensions left that I can take and they will not allow me to take them so that I can catch up on the payments. I asked about modifying the car loan and got the runaround. First, I was told that I couldn't do as such because I had not been paying on the loan with them for a sufficient amount of time. I was able to prove them wrong with this by pulling up my BK7 documents through PACER and reading to them exactly when my loan was sold to them and how long I had been making payments with them. Well after that, I was asked if the loan was modified, would I be able to make the payments. I said yes thinking they were going to help me. Well, as of two weeks ago, I do not qualify for a modification because I am so far behind in payments.

14. Fast forward to August 28, 2012, my car was repossessed at 11:19pm. I had not heard or been able to reach Crescent Bank in previous days due to Hurricane Isaac. Anyway, I got a call the same day from them offering a redemption if I pay the $1,955 (including the $355 repo fee) by Sept. 9th, 2012. When I talked with the redemption specialist about the fact that I had set up a payment arrangement in order to make partial payments weekly, I was told that they do not accept partial payments at all! So that means that the representative (Kafayat **) that I had been talking to all along was lying about the partial payments being sufficient!

15. This is the most shady, unprofessional bank I have ever dealt with. I just got my car last week and they are already giving me a hard time. My first payment has not even come yet and MJ keeps calling and harassing me every day. She is a ball buster and is going out of her way to give me a hard time. Everything she asks for I sent in (proof of residency, paystub, MV forms) & she rejects. She had the nerve to ask for my neighbors' numbers to call them and called my job and references already. Like I said, I have not even received my first bill! Dealing with this bank is already a nightmare and I'm afraid what the next 48 months are going to be like.

16. I purchased a car from Natchitoches Ford in Louisiana on March 29, 2013, a Ford Fiesta, and two months later, before paying the third note, I had to put it in the shop for transmission problems. It's been in the shop at the place I bought it from since July 17. Crescent Bank knows about it

and no one is trying to work with me on the matter. I asked to get into another vehicle of the same price or a used car of equal value, and Ford told me the only way they can help me is if I was to come up with $7000 out of pocket along the new car rebate. I feel that this is unjust to me as a customer because Crescent Bank is looking for their payment and I can't get any answers and I haven't had my car for a whole month.

17. I purchased a P.T. Cruiser 05 in 2012, which was financed through another company, who sold my contract to this sorry excuse of a business. A year later 2013 to the date, the car started to have problems. Timing belt broke after getting that fixed which cost me $489.00 for the repair. 3 months later in October the transmission is gone. 4 days later I lost my job. I called the company to inform them of the situation & for them to come & get the car. They told me they would come & get the car because of the mileage & the mechanical problems. Now when I purchased this car the mileage was 99,000 & now the mileage is 116,000. So I wanted see if my payments could be reduced to $200 a month. I was told yes & that I had to send (fax) a copy of my separation notice, the estimate for the repair and they would have no problem helping since I have never been late. Faxed everything, called to see if they had received & was told no, and faxed it 2 more times one person said on the other said yes. Now the manager of my account said I didn't send it in early enough, but no time frame was given & anyway I faxed the day after we talked each time. Then C begins to tell me that they do not refinance & that I would have to still make the payments. I asked about having a payment put at the end & was told I would still

have to a payment. Told them I could only afford to pay 1/2 $176. That's fine, he said. They got that payment & told me I would still need to make the other 1/2 for the so-called extension. Out of work for 4 months, make a payment when I can. Right now I am a month behind & they call me EVERYDAY TWICE A DAY. Sometimes when I answer they don't respond & all I hear is typing and background convo. They asked the same question each time they call or you call them. Get nasty, argue with & sometimes screams. Threaten to take further action but will not come & get the car. Call you a liar. I made a Western Union payment 2 day service. They called me 4 times saying they haven't received it. They said they called Western Union & was told a payment was not made. I called Western Union & was told the payment was there & would be available @4:46pm which makes it 48 hours. I can't understand if I talked to Jim on Monday why is someone calling me on Tuesday & days after? They say they have the RIGHT to call every day until a payment is made. This company is a nightmare! I want to seek representation because I know they have to be breaking some type of law.

Als Teara of Albany, GA

18. This company never reports the correct information to your credit report, my account is paid every month before time and on my credit report, it shows I'm late every month. I owe $2990.00 on my balance but my credit report shows I owe over $3,700. Even though I'm way ahead, my payments are $400.00 a month but I pay $450.00 a month. They will call me to tell me I have a payment due. After I tell them I am ahead on my payments, they apologize only for someone else to call me. I mostly ignore the call and

when I do, they will run a credit report to make sure my information is correct making my score go down. When you call to speak to someone, they have to ask you 101 questions to only transfer you to someone else to ask you the same damn questions over again. Jon of Bixby, OK on April 21, 2014

19. I have had tons of issues with this poor excuse for a "company", including being called a lying **, having my family constantly harassed and lied to (I even have a brother who no longer speaks to me). But all of this is nothing compared to when I made a $2500 advanced payment. I wasn't working so I prepaid for 8 months in advance and changed my due date in person at the downtown branch. 3 weeks later, I had a repossession man at my door. I called daily to point out their mistake, that I had prepaid. 2 weeks later, it was the same thing. This happened twice a month for months. 3 months later, the money I gave them has been applied to fees and fines for money I ALREADY gave them and now I owe. This CANNOT be legal and there has to be some recourse for this. I did the right thing and paid my bill, IN ADVANCE. I ended up losing the car because they refused to admit their mistakes and reverse ANY fees. I am seeking counsel, but beware... DO NOT SIGN AN ARBITRATION AGREEMENT. This doesn't allow you to file a class action lawsuit. I don't believe I signed such an agreement and need to jump on a class action lawsuit. I have payment printouts and receipts as well as numerous recordings of phone calls with them where CBT admits to blatant wrongdoing.

20. We have had our loan for just over 1 year and never been 30 days late. We have been a few days late a couple of times due to the dates that my checks fall on and have received calls from them before and after the due dates along with family members. Constantly getting calls from them even when we are not 1 day late. I have tried to speak to several reps about our account and consistently get yelled at and been cursed at more than once. We have always paid more than the monthly payment and after looking at my credit report, it shows I still owe the same amount as what we started out the loan with. I asked how this is possible after making monthly payments + extra and was told it's all interest and that the additional was not going towards the principal. So my $300+ monthly payments are just interest and at this rate I will never pay off the loan. I have researched online and found that they have had a class action lawsuit against them and I may be calling this attorney to get clarification on the lawsuit and possibly pursue legal action. I purchased my vehicle in 2012 and was told that in 6 months I could refinance to get lower payments. This was not the case. After that timeframe they told me that they don't refinance and that I would continue to pay the high note that I have. I moved nine months ago for my job and it caused a hardship. I can say that I've had issues with getting the note paid by the day, but it does get paid. They call not only me but my friends and family several times a day leaving nasty threats that I must call. We've told them numerous times that I work during the day and can't answer the phone, but it doesn't stop them from calling over 10 times in a day. I was here for about a month and my car note was 26 days late; a tow truck showed up and took my car. To get it back, I not only had to pay the note, but I had to pay two notes, tow

fees, then get to pick up the car and had to pay another storage fee and all. It was horrible. They then turned around and called me 10 days later that I was due. In December I decided that I was going to let the car go and just start over. I couldn't take the stress any longer. I took my tags off and said come get it. Three weeks later, my friend in my home state calls and said that someone was there to get the car. They were 800 miles away. I was sitting in snow and they showed up elsewhere. Anyway, another month goes by and I decided that since it was still in my drive that I would pay the notes that were due and just start looking to trade it. They told me that my pay off is the same as the amount due.

21. This company never reports the correct information to your credit report, my account is paid every month before time and on my credit report, it shows I'm late every month. I owe $2990.00 on my balance but my credit report shows I owe over $3,700. Even though I'm way ahead, my payments are $400.00 a month but I pay $450.00 a month. They will call me to tell me I have a payment due. After I tell them I am ahead on my payments, they apologize only for someone else to call me. I mostly ignore the call and when I do, they will run a credit report to make sure my information is correct making my score go down.

22. On April 18, at 9:30 pm, there was a knock at my door. Standing there were 2 guys saying they had an order to take my truck. I stood there with my mouth open. Crescent Bank had just taken over my loan because First State Bank's auto division went out of business. First State Bank had my loan for over 3 1/2 yrs. When I asked why the repo guy could not say, all he did was tell me he had to take my

truck and it was typically because of non-payment. I had proof of my payments, but he did not want to see them and took my truck! I called the bank in the morning and was greeted with nothing but rudeness and was told that their system was down and they could not check my account! I called an hour later and got the same thing! This went on for a full day! When I finally was able to speak to someone, they insisted I did not pay my March payment.

Meanwhile, I contacted the credit union who sends out my payments each month for me and pulled a 13-month history of payments, including 2 full payments in the month of November to First State Bank and every payment to Crescent Bank since they took over the loan in December of 2011. I faxed them the payment receipt as did an attorney I had called to assist me with this, since I was getting nowhere on my own and my truck was in some repo lot! When they saw proof of the March payment, they then changed it to I missed my April payment. Again, proof of that payment was shown and happened to have been cashed the day they took my truck! That story then changed to I owed them a $98.00 payment. It blossomed from there with story after story as to why they felt they had the right to take my truck.

I had then been advised by my attorney to call the bank on April 20 and make a payment of $98 that they said I owed the cost of the fee to release my truck and I would be given my truck. I called and spoke to Tanisha ** who not only was rude, but also demanded I pay my April payment because they say they didn't get it, the $98 and the fee to release the truck from the repo lot! Meanwhile, my attorney had already spoken to people there and the agreement was made and proof was sent that I paid my April payment. I did not get my truck back until April 27 after contacting and involving the institution of finance who oversees banks and insisting that someone please call the bank and find out what the hell is going on!

Crescent Bank & Trust needs to be shut down or they need to investigate their staff for embezzlement because someone is making money off of us! I just recently called to get my pay off on the truck, thinking it was around $13,000 because I have been paying on it for 4 years at $556/month - that's over $26,000 and they are telling me my balance is still over $20,000! I am hoping for satisfaction with the attorney I met; otherwise, I wish we could file a class action suit against this bank because they are terrible and someone is making money! I am hoping for satisfaction for this inconvenience and embarrassment.

23. When you call to speak to someone, they have to ask you 101 questions to only transfer you to someone else to ask you the same damn questions over age I got a new loan in 2013 from Crescent Bank for a 2013 Camaro. A payment that was 30 days late yet cost me $2173.86 for a $513.41 car note. They had the car repossessed stating it was a new loan and they could take the car back. They should have charged me a $25 late fee. Instead I had to pay to get the

car out of the pound and pay a lot of fees totaling over $2100. This bank is a joke and they call everyone and tell them your business - so unprofessional, and the CSRs are rude. You also have to give all of the same information to different people. UGH so over this financial facility. Never again.

24. As many others I am on a fixed income. When I purchased my vehicle I paid $16,000 cash, on a $25,000 used vehicle, the remainder $8,000 was financed through Crescent Bank. At first things were well and after 2 yrs I tried to get information of how much my pay off was and most times they would not give me the information, call this number or that number, or because your payment was late we can't give you the information. Then one morning while getting my children ready for school, one by one my neighbors knocked at my door with a name and a number for me to call. It was Crescent Bank. They had somehow contacted neighbors that I didn't even know their names. Results - well let's just say that never happened again. This is my fourth year curious to know the payoff because after June I will not pay another dime.

25. These people are professional crooks and scammers. How in the world are they still allowed to be in business? I asked over and over for a record from them to show all my payments and they said, "Okay, you need to make a payment to get current and we will send it to you." I said, "But I don't owe you anything; the car is paid off!" They said. "No, you owe $7000." I say, "Okay, I'll make one payment and you can refund it to me when you see my payments are all made." They say, "Sure, no problem", and then they take my money and never send my report. The

next month comes, it's the same story. "You are behind on a payment make that payment and we will send you whatever you need". I make another payment and again nothing.

26. I finally quit paying them and they have tried to repossess my car but can't get to it due to location. I have contacted several attorneys but can't get anyone to take my case... Beware of Crescent Bank of New Orleans. They are professional thieves and they will take you! \

27. I Have been paying my car loan for six years. They always charge me a late fee because my loan was due on the 4th of each month. I ask them to change due date but they said they couldn't so therefore, my payment was always late. In July 2010, they offered me a plan that I could pay a certain amount of money for June and July 2010, and it would mean my loan would be paid off in August 2011. I continue to make my regular payment.

28. Crescent Bank & Trust is a company that have people working for them and they don't do nothing but ** people and their credit. I have asked Mr. Vince what can they do about my credit report and he stated nothing. This is not fair; if it's easy to put a negative on your credit then they should be able to rectify their mess. The reason: lates"were put on my credit per Vince is that the system was showing the modification amount of $317.00 was a partial payment of the $442. This is crazy. I have the paperwork that I faxed in March showing my new amount of $317. they have a

glitch in their system, they need to fix it and I want my credit to be fixed by Crescent Bank & Trust. Lastly, I requested Mr. ***** to send me paperwork that they have credited me the late fees and I have yet to receive it to this day. They did a new modification on 10/29 and my new amt is $323.18. I want my credit corrected!

29. gust 2011, when my loan matured, they said I still owe $500. So I made an arrangement with Tiffany to make payments. She agreed and I sent them $50 for September and October. I received a phone call from Ms. ** who informed me she was now handling my account and my payments weren't agreeable any more. So she said that they would do a modification of my past due plus late fees totaling $1400. I told her I was not signing any more forms with her but would pay the $118 per month. She said I couldn't do that and the company would take further action. I said," Fine, I'm tired of arguing." I don't work. I'm on a fixed income but I have paid this loan to the last month. Why are they so mean? Can you help me?

30. Bought a new vehicle in 2008, it was for 66 months. The payments were no problem as I put a large down payment on it. My problem with them is the hoops you have to jump thru to make a phone payment or ask them a question in general; they give you the third degree asking about 20 questions that they say is relevant to the loan. This is not true cause after 2 times I refused to answer any questions they just put you on hold a little longer. I was late 1 time in 66 months and paid the late fee, however I did use the grace period a lot of times, not knowing if I did more

interest would accrue, so I was shocked to learn my final payment was $200.00 more than my regular payment all because they said I was using the grace period during the life of the loan. My payment was due on the 6th and late on the 16th, it only exceeded the 16th once, but the other 65 times it was paid between the 1st and 16th so $200.00 for using the grace period is just b/s fees in my opinion. It seems this company will screw you every chance they get. I am glad this car is paid off and will never use them again.

31. In 2009 I needed to buy a new vehicle. I admit that my credit is not the greatest but I had just received back payment for disability. I put $6,000 down payment on the vehicle. The rest was financed through Crescent Bank and Trust. I receive my Disability check once a month and never on the same date. This bank started calling me one day after payment was due right from the first. A few of the things they wanted me to do was: 1) Borrow the money till my check came in, 2) Post date a check, 3) Give them payment over the phone which adds on more charges. I was recently in the emergency room for breathing problems and received a call from them. The person on the line wanted me to call my bank to stop payment on a lost check in the mail and give them a payment over the phone. When I ask if I could call them back after I got out of the ER, they were insistent that I call my bank. I will never deal with this bank again. Any action taken against this company, I would be happy to add my name to the list.

32. If I knew then what I know now about this company and their employees, I would have NEVER EVER done any business with them. It's bad enough I get called sometime 6

times a day with reminder calls before my payment was ever due, I recently in a one-hour time span received 40 missed calls, them calling almost every minute on the minute, I had just spoken with them 3 days prior due to only paying $300 of my $366 payment due to job loss letting them know the situation..And trust me I have all the phone logs to back this up. Their employees are super RUDE no matter what you call them for or vice versa as well as the education level and grammar sucks. You can't half understand the messages they leave. I have now contacted an attorney due to the harassment, by the FTC Fair Debit Act (see # five from the FTC below); they cannot harass someone to that extent... I can assure you I plan to take this as far as possible to see something done about such a shady company and plan to make sure I get as much info out to other consumers to warn them of this GOD AWFUL Company.

33. I will admit I fell behind in my payments slow payments. I was recently at the tail end of my nursing program. I kept in contact was never disrespectful to any of the employees. I explained that I was waiting on my first pay check that I was not sure how much the check would be but I did know it would be a live check... (not direct deposit). Any time I had always paid current. They began threnting my with repossession. I explain if they had to take that action (I did not want that I am close to having the car paid for) I would not try to fight of hide the vehicle. I would rather try to get a payment in and I borrowed money from a payday advance... They still sent a guy out to "inspect the vehicle after I made my car payment for the previous month (May I paid this on June 19th) I

explain my June's payment would be paid 6/28! I wanted to keep my car.

34. Today I called my payment in after a 12hr shift. They accepted it, I asked them if I was still under a volunteer repossession...the rep said no. they have been rude...I explained the reason for my constant calls are because I have been lied too by them and I was not going to make another payment unless I had "proof" they refused to send me anything in writing about my balance and refused to email me a currant statement the online site still shows I have a balance!

35. My car was repossessed on Wednesday night. I didn't know until Thursday morning. When I called them, I was told that I needed to fax them over the information they requested with the money sent via Western Union. I faxed them all the information they needed on Friday and I was told that my license was illegible. I faxed it over again and they said no problem. I made the payment on Tuesday (Monday was Memorial Day) and they said my license was still illegible. It is Wednesday and I still haven't been able to get my car back. My account manager is Kafayat; she is very inadequate. I asked to speak to her supervisor but they don't tell me her name. I keep on getting the runaround, and meanwhile my car is in storage and I can't pick it up although I made my payment. I know I was late with my payment but this is no way to treat me. I can't wait to finish with this bank. 3 more months and I'm done with them. I never paid late except for this time. This is TERRIBLE!!! ALL BEWARE of this company!

36. Research your options for loans before doing business with Crescent Bank & Trust. I like many, lost my home due to the economy in 2009 and my credit took a huge hit. I was in need of a new vehicle and was approved for a loan with Crescent Bank and Trust, to whom I knew nothing about, except that they were willing to carry my loan for the purchase. Short and sweet, I pay or I request the additional money I pay over my payment each much, usually a hundred or more, be applied to the principle of the balance of the loan. After almost 2 years of making my payments, this company still applies the extra money toward my next payment! This only increases the amount of INTEREST they are able to collect from me. This company is a total rip off, with poor customer service, and charging fee's any where they can. As stated in another complain, they charge $8.95 to collect a payment, which is silly. What is going on when people what to charge you to make a payment?? Research your options before doing business with this Bank, or they will take you to the Bank!!! My car was financed through Crescent Bank and Trust back in 2007. My car was suppose to be paid off May 2011 so I called to get the payoff. That was the last coupon in the book payment 42. I was told that I owe 4 more payments. So I contacted the bank manager they are trying to say that my account was 43 days past due. I have made all my payments on time. I have received harassing phone calls every day since April 2010. They even call my mother every day. I received a statement last week of my payments I have made 45 payments and they still say that I owe 4 more payments. The loan amount that was

financed was 11,000 I have paid almost 19,000 and they expect me to pay another 2400.00. I noticed on the statements when extra money was paid it was posted to my account. I don't owe them anything thing else but they expect me to pay 3 more payments and I have used all the coupons in the book. I don't owe them anything else and I don't know what to do.

37. I purchased a car in May 2012 from Sonny's of Shelby, NC. The car was financed through Sunray Financial in Hickory, NC but I could walk into Sonny's and make my car payment. In August of 2013, I was informed that Sonny's would be closing and that Crescent Bank and Trust would be taking over my account. That's when the problems started. Crescent Bank harassed me stating I was one payment behind and wanted me to make this payment ASAP because it could affect my credit score. Since I purchased this vehicle, I have never missed a payment. I now have my payment history to prove it. But anyway, my vehicle was equipped with a tracking system which sounds an alarm to remind you when your payment is due and if your payment is not made within 24 hours, the vehicle will shut down. In order to prevent your vehicle shutting down, you need a pass code to input into the system, which you normally get when you make your payment. I called Crescent Bank on 12/31/2013 to make my payment for December which was due on the 30th. I was informed that one was available in the department for me to speak with so I wouldn't be able to make my payment. Mind you this is New Year's Eve so they would be closed the next day which was New Year's Day, so I would have to wait and make my payment on January 2, 2014. I called in to make

my payment on January 2, and was told the department I needed to speak with was not available, but she could take my payment. After making the payment, I told the Rep I needed a pass code to keep my vehicle from shutting down. Her response to that was "What is a pass code?" I explained to her what it was and she told me to hold on. She came back to the phone and told me that she would send an email to the department I needed in regards to the pass code and that someone would call me back. I explained to her that my car may shut down at 5:00 so I needed to have someone call me back ASAP. No one has called me back yet and I have called Crescent Bank 8-10 times between Jan 2-3 and keep getting the same response. There is no one available in the department you need to speak with. My car shut down on my daughter yesterday 45 minutes away from home and now I can't get a pass code to restart it. Today is Friday and if I don't get a pass code before 5:00, I will be without a car all weekend. I have already missed two days of work due to this and my daughter had to miss work today because this is our only means of transportation.

38. Why would you take over accounts if you can meet the consumer needs once they make a payment? Ever since I had to make my first payment to Crescent Bank in September, I have always had trouble getting a pass code. I have been told that they were sending someone out to remove the pass code system from the vehicles, this has not happened. I was also told that they were giving pass codes valid for ninety days, this is not true either. I spoke to a rep last week and she said they couldn't even get pass codes anymore. If that is true, then what am I to do? I could understand if I my payment had not been made, but like I

said I have never missed a payment since I purchased this vehicle.

39. I am so over them... My loan was sold to them and it has been hell ever since! I lost my job and my new job pay dates changed They told me that I was only allowed one due date change per the lifetime of the loan! I am like life happens and you all act like these things don't happen... I am so over them!

40. Every time I have communicated with the customer service reps they're so rude and mean like you owe them personally. They make it hard to make arrangements. Really trying to literally bully you. If they haven't received your car payment two days past the due date, here comes the harassment. Those calls can't be recorded the way they talk to you. If so I know they would be fired unless that's how the owners want their company ran. I'm trying so hard to get refinanced. I had such a bad experience with them that I looked online for reviews and up and behold. What have I gotten myself into? Should have checked the website before I signed that contract. CONSUMERS PLEASE BEWARE OF CRESCENT BANK & TRUST.

41. I have had my loan with CB&T for 18 months. I have never....NEVER.... been 30 days late. I have been days late and I always included late fees with those payments. I have recently been alerted by a credit profile service I am enrolled in that they have run hard copy references on my report twice this year... hence lowering my credit score. I

am positive they have done this to all of you as well. A hard copy requires the signature of the person who holds that social security number. I did include communication with my last payment forewarning them of possible legal action if it happens again. But, once is enough. Why are we on a sub-prime loan? Poor/average credit. This is just wrong in all aspects! If anyone else is interested in signing on, please contact me. I will find us a lawyer and carry this out.

42. Owed 2 months sent in m.o they say they didn't receive even though postal service sent me copy of signature of who received it. Car repossessed, paid all fees. Months later have balance of over $1000 was told the fees I paid was placed by mistake on principal so now I need to pay that again. Finished paying for car after 60 months, no discount for fees applied to principal. Now owe over $1700, paid and balance $1300. Was told to pay $975 and call it quits. Couldn't afford to so I paid $500 on Friday with $800 balance, car repossessed again on Sunday. I refuse to pay another repossession fee. So thanks to Crescent Bank and Trust, I lost my car for $800.... Wow.... where do we get these dishonest people from? I am sad will get another car someday though.

43. My car was financed with Crescent Bank and Trust. I was late 1 payment, so it was repo. In the State of IL the finance company has to tell the consumer where the vehicle is located, because the personal property inside the car does not belong to the finance company. They keep calling me and they are calling my family members, they already have

the vehicle, I told them keep it. I'd rather have a bad mark on my credit than deal with them.

44. I ** hate these this Bank. Very rude and unprofessional. I am looking forward to refinancing and moving to a different bank! Humanity is lost with this company.

45. I recently got laid off and started working again a month later. Yet I have a huge pay cut so my time frame of making my payments are well off the due date scale by about a week or two. I receive a call every month from female reps about my account. I tell the reps my intended time frame on when I am going to send my payment by money order (including late fees) AND I call to tell when I have actually dropped the payment in the mailbox to head their way. I called to ask for the bank to send me a statement of my car note so I can have an agency help me out to pay them and I needed it by Wednesday morning (it was Monday morning). They told me it would take 24 to receive the fax. I asked if they could email it. They said no but they could only send me a payment history printout and not a statement.

46. I give them two fax numbers, 24 hours roll by, no fax. 48 hours roll by and still no fax. I go to the website, make an account to check my account and print the due amount sheet for the agency. I called and asked them about the missing fax. The female rep says their fax machine was down and that there was a different department that handles those types of request. I get to the agency take care of the

business. I get the call saying your fax has made it - AFTER THE APPOINTMENT. So this last time I called and spoke with a male rep. I told him I have sent my past due amount in by mail (including late fee) AND my next payment [(which will be on time) WITH NO LATE FEE. He had the audacity to tell me that my payment was unacceptable because I was 21 days late on my last payment. So I said, "Excuse me"!! Then asked, "So are you saying you are going to refuse my payments?" He said, "I am saying it is unacceptable for you to send your payment almost a month late.".

47. My daughter's car was repossessed by CB&T because she was behind in her payments. We contacted CB&T and spoke with Sarah and Jamie, paid almost $1,600 and were told they would fax us information that needed to be completed. We went to a UPS store and waited and waited for the fax, called them back and they said it was sent but they would send again. I waited and waited again, called back again, and on and on and on. We finally discovered that they were trying to fax the information to my cell phone. I called them again and they again tried to fax to my cell phone. We finally got them to use the right fax number, and then filled out the paperwork, provided copies of everything they asked for, and tried to fax back. First fax number, we got a message that said the number was disconnected. Second fax number, we got their phone greeting, tried again and got someone's personal voicemail. We tried again and got a communication error.

48. We called again to speak with Jamie, my daughter's account rep, who gave us an email address to scan and send the paperwork to. We asked Jamie to call us if they did not get the email or if there were any problems with the paperwork. Jamie then told us to call back at 4:00 to check on the status of everything. When we called back at 4:00, we were told by Sarah, who said she was Jamie's supervisor, that Jamie had left, and didn't we realize that they were on Eastern time and it was 5:00 there? Well, no, we didn't. Sarah then said they had never gotten the emailed information, told us we weren't Jamie's only account and we shouldn't expect her to get back with us, etc. Sarah then said she couldn't talk to me about the account anymore because my daughter was not there (funny, I had been talking to both her and Jamie all day about the account). I conference my daughter in. Sarah told us there was nothing we could do and we just needed to keep trying the fax. All this time, my daughter is without her car and we have paid everything they said we owed, including repo fees.

49. When I asked Sarah for the name of the company president and the corporate headquarters' number, she refused to give me the name and said that I had called the corporate headquarters. She would not give me a direct line number to corporate, and would not give me the name of any of the officers of the bank. I was finally transferred to Danielle, who gave me her email address and told me to scan and email the documents to her. Of course, she never received them, although when I scanned them, I also emailed them to myself and I received them just fine. I then tried to forward the email I got off the scanned documents, which

of course they again never received. My daughter was then told there was nothing else they could do and we'd have to keep trying the fax. Again, my daughter has no transportation and the car is sitting in an impound lot that charges a daily fee.

50. I finally got a confirmation page from the fax, so we called again to make sure they got it. This is over four hours of work, 16 calls on my cell phone, plus calls from my work phone, house phone, and my daughter's fiancé's cell phone. We got probably the only bright spot in that whole company, a rep named Megan who confirmed for us that the fax was received. Megan also told us that they needed a copy of our insurance Declaration's Page, not the insurance card. It makes sense. But every time we talked to Sarah and Jamie and told them we were sending a copy of the insurance card, we were told that was what they needed. Megan also told us that they only have two fax lines and that emails from outside the company take a very long time to get through. What a way to run a business! We have to call them again in the morning and let our account rep, Jamie, know that receipt of all documents was confirmed and that we were told it would only take an hour to review the docs, then a few hours in the repo department, and we should be able to get the car tomorrow. I have no doubt, however, that when we call Jamie, the story will be different.

51. Also, my daughter was told that if she did not have the payment and paperwork by Friday, the car would be sent to

auction. They are now denying that they ever said that, but I heard the conversation myself and that is exactly what they said. When Sarah tried to deny it and said that they recorded every conversation, I told her to go ahead and pull the recordings so we could listen to them. Of course, that has not happened. Also, my daughter made a payment a few months ago, and then they called her fiancé the next day and told him they were behind one payment and they were going to pick up the car. When he told them that my daughter had made the payment, they said, "Oh, are both of you on the same account? We thought this was two different cars." My daughter got herself in this position, but nobody deserves to go through this garbage for over four hours. If you are currently dealing with Crescent Bank & Trust, you have my deepest sympathy. If you are thinking about dealing with Crescent Bank & Trust, run away and don't look back.

52. give Crescent Bank and Trust a zero. The staff at this company is apparently miserable and incompetent. They lie, transfer you to different departments and aren't willing to give you clarification when you request documentation or an explanation. They are so beyond rude; they try to fast talk you off the phone and don't listen to your concerns. They dismiss whatever you have to say which all results in frustration. My requests for a copy of my contract and an explanation of the charges not reflected on my vehicle purchase agreement were dismissed. The rude idiots', both male and female, unprofessional tone created tension and arguments with these people who answer the phone at this company. I'm a grown woman and when someone yells at me because they are miserable working at this company so

they take it out on customers, I don't tolerate that so I yell right back. Then I'm told I don't need to yell or use profanity. These people aren't properly trained and most likely don't have a secondary education or even a GED. Cory **, go jack off somewhere. Everyone else whose names I didn't get while trying to resolve my issues, kick rocks!

53. The employees at Crescent Bank & Trust are the rudest and unprofessional people I have ever encountered. I had a change in employment and they were not willing to wait one day for the payment. They were sending a repo person for my truck as we were speaking on the phone. If I had the money, I would pay this truck off in full. If anyone ever mentioned Crescent Bank to me, I will take off and run.

54. I purchased a car with a subprime loan through Crescent Bank and Trust. After several months, I asked why my balance and interest was so high. The friendly service rep, Theva, told me that I had been a payment behind from the onset of the loan. I told her that I had sent the payment early, because I had been through a divorce and did not have great credit and was trying to rebuild. I also wondered why no one had told me after almost a year. Interest had accrued astronomically and calls were constant. Since then, I have been trying to get verification of all payments. My payments would be deducted from my credit union account. The credit union has since merged and my account was closed. I am threatened w/ repossession when I am 30 days past due. I do not believe that they would let me pay a note two months behind on a new loan without calling or writing.

55. Nitza of West Orange, NJ

I have a car loan with this company. My original car loan was with Key Bank and Trust who sold all of their car loans to Crescent. I will start by saying that with Key my vehicle was repossed once close to when I first brought it. I will admit I did not have a steller payment record. Scince Crescent took over my vehicle has been repossed three times. The first time was valid. The second time they said that if two months are owed then they would come and take the car. This third time was 10/31 at 3am.

I was confused as to why the car was being taken because I had just made a payment. I made a payment on 10/28 using Money Gram in the amount of $380 (for Sep) I called Crescent around 9:30 and spoke to Richard. He told me that the last payment he saw was on Oct 4. I gave him the Money Gram reference number and he did see the payment. He said there should be no problem he would talk to his supervisor and I would not have to pay any repossession fees.

Richard called me back at 11:30am and told me that he thought his supervisor could do more and that I had to pay a $445 repossession fee and Oct payment to get my car back. I asked him why the payment was not posted to my account and he explained that he did not know and that I should have called them with the reference number. HE gave me his supervisor's number. I called Mark Moticheck and he told me that this should teach me a lesson.

I asked him why the payment had not gone through and he said that my account had been blocked from payments on Friday 10/27.

I asked what did that mean did that just mean that the payment I made was floating around and he said yes. I do not dispute that I was late the problem that I have is that no one can explain why the Money Gram payment did not post.

When I expressed concern that this is an electronic payment Mark insisted it was not. However on the company web site it lists Money Gram as an electronic payment. I just do not understand why I have to pay a $447 repossession fee for a payment which was never posted to my account.

56. My car was stolen a few months ago and I went to Don Marshall Chrysler Center 716 Hwy 27 Somerset, KY 42501. I told them I had bad credit. They said they could help me get a car. A Don Marshall representative told me that after making 3 payments I could come back and trade in for any vehicle I wanted. they said they could only sell me this 2003 dodge caravan. they said the loan was for 18 months. (it is for 3 years) the payments were 373.99 a month.

    I didn't read the things I signed. I believed what I was told. I tried to take the van back to don marshalls and they said I have to have it for a year because I am still paying on interests. I took my van to a different dealer and they said I was really screwed and they have seen other people in my situation coming from Don Marshalls. I went home and looked at my papers and the bank is charging me 25% interest. I believe Don Marshall and Crescent Bank and Trust took advantage of me when I was in a desperate situation.

57. Yulounda of Stone Mountain, GA

On Aug. 27, 02 the bank reposed my 99 Kia, because of my paying late at the time I owed for Aug. and they said I owed $26.00 from July (which I didn't realize). After repossing the car I didn't hear from them for four months, than in Jan. 03 I had call from Ms Knight, she informed by that the car had been sole(for about $2000.00)and that I was responsible for the balance which she told me was $5000.00 something dollars.

I told Ms Knight that I hadn't heard from the bank in 4 months and that I didn't think the balance was right. Ms Knight kept asking me doesn't mean that I was not going to pay? and I told her I would like something in writing and that I would be contracting a lawyer to see what my rights were. After contracting the lawyer, who told me to get something in writing and see about setting up a payment plan, I than called Ms Knight back, she told me that she would pass the message on to the bank lawyer.
I did send the bank a $50.00 check, to hold them until my lawyer and my credit counselor could contact them, they return the check. I suffer from uncontrolled high blood pressure and depression, this has been very hard they threaten to garish my wage or put a lien on my home.

58. **AUTHOR`S OWN CASE:**

SUPERIOR COURT OF THE STATE OF CALIFORNIA

COUNTY OF LOS ANGELES, SOUTHEAST DISTRICT, LIMITED CIVIL

EMMANUEL ADETULA VS CRESCENT BANK & TRUST

Case No. 12CT3326

EMMANUEL ADETULA ("Defendant/Cross-Complainant" hereby denies all allegations made by the Plaintiff in this case. ("Defendant/ Complainant "herein) is making a cross-complain because a serious intent to agree with the Defendant/Cross-Complainant needs was not present from the Auto dealer "National wide Auction Systems" , therefore to a reasonable person , the sales contract (EXHIBIT A) presented by the Plaintiff was a surprising used car sales agreement that involve used **auto dealer fraud**, **deception** , **unfair business practice** and consumer fraud by the auto dealer . The action of the dealer was an intentional violation of the California Fair Business Practices Act therefore the Defendant/Cross-Complainant is requesting the court to award punitive damages in the sum of $100,000 against the dealer; Nationwide Auction System & Finance and the Plaintiff in this case; Crescent Bank & Trust for the following reasons.

FACT 1. Non-Disclosure of Salvage Title

I Emmanuel Adetula, the Defendant/Cross-

Complainant told the dealer that I needed a reliable car. I asked if the specific car had ever been wrecked. Though the paint looked new. The dealer responded that the car had not been wrecked and that he had had the car repainted because the paint had faded. The dealer told me the car had not been wrecked that is why I agreed to pay $8,892.08 for the car with all interest , but within few months of paying for the car I learned that the car had been salvaged and a salvage title had been issued. The dealer duped me into signing documents to allow for a state inspection and the dealer obtains a rebuilt title which was auto dealer fraud, I was on the way to return the vehicle , but the dealer promised me he would refinance the vehicle for me and give me a new vehicle one year after I have pay for the car for a year and use it to increase my fico score and credit ratings, , but after the agreed date I went to the dealer for replacing the vehicle, the dealer has shut down his business location and sold the loan to Crescent Bank & Trust, and the used auto dealer auction site has been leased to a trailer park business, so I had nothing else to do than to be negotiating with the Plaintiff " Crescent Bank & Trust" who then became a new Auto financing bank , that was not the first auto financier that I signed the loan with at a time of the EXHIBIT 1 agreement between me and the dealer, the Plaintiff bought the loan, and he has no history of the condition of the vehicle in this case, so at a time the Exhibit A agreement was entered into between me and the dealer " NATIONWIDE AUTO SYSTEMS" the Plaintiff "CRESCENT BANK & TRUST" was not a part of the auto loan financing agreement.

The loan was bought in the secondary market by the Plaintiff, the condition of the vehicle was never known to the Plaintiff, The action of the dealer was an intentional violation of the California Fair Business Practices Act therefore I am requesting the court to award a punitive damages in the amount of $100,000 against the dealer and the Plaintiff in this case.

FACT 2. The Dealer had placed a window sticker on the car representing that the car had a remaining factory warranty. After I discovered problems with the car, I sought warranty work on the car. I was informed that the car warranty was voided. The dealer was no longer in business or has since moved out of southern California location and it was the Plaintiff only that I have access to on phone, I am in CALIFORNIA, the bank is in another state, and the Plaintiff cannot solve my problem with the car, than to negotiate low monthly payment with me from $367 to $155 a month for non-operational vehicle. The Federal Trade Commission enacted the FTC Buyer's Guide Regulations which require that each used car offered for sale contain prominently and conspicuously on the vehicle so that both sides are readily readable, A "Buyer's Guide", also known as a window sticker. The Buyer's Guide must include:

- The vehicle make, model, year and Vehicle Identification Number;
- The name and address of the dealer.
- A description of the meaning of "as is"
- A clear disclosure of any warranty coverage and the terms and conditions of any warranty coverage. 16 C.F.R. § 455.2.
- If the car is not covered by any warranty, either express or implied, the dealer must check the block labeled "AS-IS-NO WARRANTY." If the car is

covered by a written warranty, the dealer must check the box labeled "WARRANTY."

- The FTC Used Car Rule states that it is deceptive for a used car dealer to misrepresent the mechanical condition of a used vehicle; or, misrepresent the terms of a warranty offered in connection with the sale of a used vehicle; or, represent the used vehicle is sold with a warranty when the vehicle is sold without a warranty; or, fail to disclose, prior to sale, that a used vehicle is sold without a warranty; or, fail to make available, prior to sale, the terms of any written warranty applicable to the used vehicle. 16 C.F.R. §455.1.

FACT 3. In this case the dealer had violated this rule stated in item 2 above, by attempting to use two different window stickers, in view of the fact that the dealer had intentionally deceive me a consumer the buyer and transferred such continual deceit systems to the Plaintiff. the Car Dealer screws me and the Plaintiff continues to this day an intentional violation of the California Fair Business Practices Act with the scheme to treat a car proven piece of junk as a trade rather than a dollar for dollar collateral swap therefore I am requesting the court to award a punitive damages in the amount of

$100,000 against the Plaintiff in this case.

FACT 4. **"De-horsing" The Dealer Coercion Technique**

I went to Nationwide Auction in 2008 with $1,800 cash to buy a car at the auction , cash and carry, it was the Nationwide Salesmen at the auction that used Coercion technique to lured me into auto loan, the salesmen convinced me that with a Car loan, I can build my credit, so the only reason the car salesmen at a used car auction was able to convinced me to use the $1,800 cash in my hand as down payment to finance the car loan was to help me to build my credit, up to that point I had never bought anything on credit or loan , so I have no credit, I have no fico score, I pay cash for what I need, but the salesmen convinced me that if I buy a car on loan, paying it monthly will build my credit, and that buying cash and carry is not to my advantage, I went there to pay 100% for a used car at an auction, cash and carry and drive away, owing nobody, but a car salesman suggested financing to build good credit ratings, but Crescent Bank the auto loan financing who purchased the auto loan from Nationwide the car dealer failed to report my monthly payments to credit reporting agencies for the first 2 years of my monthly payments of the car loan, thereby destroyed by its mismanagement of loan process to consumers to damaged my credit far below the point when I signed the loan as in EXHIBIT A .

FACT 5. The Plaintiff failed to report this car loan transaction to credit report agencies and therefore failed in its banking responsibilities to consumers , It was this action of Crescent bank that prevented me from refinancing the car for a new car and pay off Crescent Bank when the car becomes nonoperational , so the Dealer "De-horsing" the car dealer coercion technique with high pressure on me consumer into buying the car on loan financing to improved my credit was defeated by the action of the Plaintiff.

It was not until I stopped paying for the nonoperational car, when the dealer was no longer around to take it back and the bank wants nothing than for me to pay up the loan. The Plaintiff then after 2 years went and reported default loan to credit agencies against my credit, which destroyed my credit, and prevented me from getting a job or house to rent from 2010 to 2012, so for the dealer to have ostensibly value the car and interest rate based on my no credit at a time of purchase and did agreed to report the payment to credit reporting agencies from the second day of EXHIBIT A , but failed to do so for 2 years, but only reported it as negative against me to intentional destroyed my credit in order to make me captive under the car loan agreement thereby continue harassing me with debt collection Strategy after coercing me to purchased the clunker car at exorbitant rates. The dealer made me as a consumer feels committed to the car and compelled me to pay more with higher interest rate of 29% but Plaintiff denied me to use it to improved my credit ratings which was the only reason I purchased the car in the first instance under auto financing, so for the dealer De-horsing" The Dealer Coercion Technique and Plaintiff failure to report it to credit reporting agencies from 2008 to 2010 until the Defendant stopped payment on the loan has caused the Defendant a personal hardship, of unemployment , homelessness because most employer refused to employ the defendant because of unpaid bad debts of $7,500 threshold , and Plaintiff report on this loan grew at 29% per month a month, and it was never stated on the credit report as a car loan but as if it was reported intentional by Crescent Bank recovery like a bankruptcy, at a time payment was stopped it was $4,228.87 but the Plaintiff continue to report increase of 29% monthly on it, until it grew up as a bigger loan that make employer and landlord to denied my jobs and apartment for rents since 2010 , therefore The action of the dealer and the Plaintiff was an intentional violation of the California Fair Business Practices Act therefore I am requesting the court to award a punitive damages against the dealer and the Plaintiff in the total amount of $100,000 while the collections request of the Plaintiff in the amount of $4,228.87, interest rate of 29% late charges pursuant to Exhibit A, Plaintiff attorney`s fees and all costs incurred and relief sought by the Plaintiff and Plaintiff Attorney be denied by this court.

FACT 6. The vehicle is not operational since 2010 , the Defendant/Cross-Complainant has donated the Vehicle to a 501 c 3 nonprofit organization as Junk car , and it is in DMV record as such, because when the Plaintiff was informed to come and repossessed the Junk Vehicle , the Plaintiff refused because Plaintiff knows that the vehicle does not worth more than $100, but want to use the court process for collection to value it for $4,228.87, with interest rate of $2,344.04, Defendant/Cross-Complainant hereby rejects motion for monetary Judgment in favor of Plaintiff/ Cross-Defendant because Plaintiff is not entitled for any damages of an account stated.

Defendant filed its Opposition to Plaintiff`s Grounds to reject Defendant`s Motion to vacate Summary Judgment that was in favor of Plaintiff AND Defendant`s request for dismissal of this case in its entirety.

I SUMMARY

Plaintiff`s Motion must be denied for one simple reason.

MEMORANDUM OF POINTS AND AUTHORITIES

Plaintiff `s Sole Contention in this case is that Plaintiff was Properly Assigned a Security Agreement, but as evidenced by the Plaintiff `s Exhibits this is not a Security Agreement nor is it a Contract , but an Auto Sales between a Buyer and a Seller in 2008 that was based on both written and verbal Agreement of which the Title of the Vehicle ; a 2002 Ford Focus Car is with DMV in the name of Cogent Financial Group to-date January 17, 2014 which is a prove that Nationwide Auction Services doing business as Cogent Financial Group that made a written and verbal agreement with the Defendant did not transferred ownership of this Vehicle to Crescent Bank & Trust who is the Plaintiff in this case, that is, Cogent Financial Group retained ownership of the Car with DMV to-date January 17, 2014, that was why when the Defendant requested the Plaintiff between 2010 to 2013 to come and repossessed the car from the Defendant, that the Vehicle was supposed to be replaced by Nationwide in 2009 under a verbal agreement made in 2008 , (this vehicle was in auto garage between 2010 to 2013 until it was towed away to a junk yard after Plaintiff refused to pick it after another request again in 2013) but Plaintiff refused to repossessed the car 2010 - 2013 because the Plaintiff realized legally it has no right to repossessed a car that does not belong to the Plaintiff, but Plaintiff Attorney relied only on fabrication of illegal security and contract documents to collect the loan balance payment of a car that does not belong to the Plaintiff he is representing as an Attorney, as evidenced on the DMV Ownership Title, Plaintiff made a false claim to the court that a security agreement or contract documents papers was assigned for debt collection , but in the past 7 years (2008-2014) Plaintiff has failed to come up with a living witness from Nationwide Auction System or Cogent Financial Group to prove to the court that it hold a legal right to this car. Plaintiff relied on written agreement as Exhibits but denied the oral agreement that such written agreement will be modified in 2009 by Nationwide Auction System, but Plaintiff continue to misled the court with a contract papers documents as Exhibits to make a collections of money of a movable property that

Plaintiff has no knowledge of whereabouts or may does not want to repossessed but just want money from the Defendant despite the fact that the verbal agreement between the Defendant and Nationwide Auction Systems becomes null and void when Nationwide went into bankruptcy in 2009 and moved out of town and therefore Nationwide failed in its obligations to replaced the vehicle as promised the Defendant in 2008. Nationwide and Cogent already considered this loan a bad loan and has written it off in its book. The economic recession of 2009 forced Nationwide or Cogent out of Los Angeles County, but Crescent Bank in its debt collection corporate schemes continues to use collection Attorney to harass the Defendant with supposed assigned security agreement while denying the ownership of the junk vehicle of which such agreement was based. Plaintiff is misusing the court process of debt collection for assigned security agreement to misstates the rules of Auto Financing and procedure on consumers ; that a Car repossession must first take place by a Borrowing Bank when the Borrower requested that he can no longer meet the obligation of a car loan monthly payment agreement, so before the bank can sue the borrower for the auto balance, attempt must have been made to take the car back from the borrower, but in a situation where the bank refused to take back or repossessed the car as the title owner with the DMV, or have written off such loan based on its own internal financial management decision , it becomes a fraudulent case for a third party like Crescent Bank & Trust the Plaintiff in this case to come up with a collection case requesting a court order for money judgment when the original title owner is nowhere to be found and has already claim such loss under a bankruptcy protection, this case is nothing but an abuse of court process . Thus, Defendant motion to vacate summary Judgment must be granted.

III CONCLUSION

Based on the foregoing, Defendant respectfully requests that all Plaintiff claims in this case be denied and that this case be dismissed in its entirety because Plaintiff claimed of assigned security Agreement does not meet the standard procedure of required evidence and witnesses as evidenced in the DMV vehicle registration even as at the date of hearing on January 17, 2014.

Dated: January 17, 2014

Emmanuel Adetula
Defendant in Proper

This Vehicle registration is registered in the name of Cogent Bank/Emmanuel Adetuls at Department of Motor Vehicle – CA DMV, the Vehicle was never transferred to Crescent Bank the Plaintiff in this case therefore all documents presented by the Attorney is a complete fabrication of lies and distortion of facts to misled the court to win this case by trick, as of May 27 2014, this Vehicle is still registered in the name of Cogent Bank and Emmanuel Adetuls, therefore for the Court to award a judgment in favor of Crescent Bank on Auto loan on a vehicle that DMV does not have a record that Crescent Bank is the owner on Title is improper, how can you say somebody is owing you on a vehicle loan , but another bank name is on title with DMV , if a auto loan has been purchased by Crescent Bank from Cogent bank , why is it that the title of the vehicle not released to Crescent bank on DMV records? . how did Crescent bank purchased auto loan, and claimed it has no responsibility to repossessed the car when the borrower failed to pay the car notes?, but how Crescent bank can easily go to court, filed a case, get judgment, then filed the judgment with Los Angeles county recorder`s office to put a lien on the auto borrower`s home in Los Angeles? that is because the judicial process in Los Angeles County is based on dancing between the Judge and the Attorney on this case? Below is the DMV registration of this vehicle to-date May 27, 2014 with other proof that Crescent Bank and its Attorney rejected all offer to come and pick up this car from the Defendant in this case, but tricked the court to received a favorable judgment to put a lien on a home of the Defendant. Only in Los Angeles County this can happen, everywhere in America, Crescent bank is already known as fraud.

* INCOMPLETE APPLICATION**SEE ABOVE**THIS IS NOT AN OPERATING PERMIT *

MAKE	YR MODEL	YR 1ST SOLD	VLF CLASS	YR	TYPE VEH	TYPE LIC	LICENSE NUMBER
FORD	2002	2002	BN	2008	12S	11	6UVY229

BODY TYPE MODEL: SW · MP: G · MO: VS · VEHICLE/VESSEL ID NUMBER: 1FAHP36372W239326

TYPE VEHICLE/VESSEL USE: AUTOMOBILE · DATE ISSUED: 05/27/14 · CC/ALCO: 19 · DT FEE RECVD: 05/27/14 · PIC: 0

RDF REASONS: 0 D

R/O
ADETULS EMMANUEL
14717 HAWTHORNE BLVD #B
LAWNDALE
CA 90260

AMOUNT PAID $ 97.00

AMOUNT DUE $ 97.00
AMOUNT RECVD
CASH : 40.00
CHCK :
CRDT : 60.00
CASH BACK : 3.00

L/O
COGENT FNCL GRP
PO BX 6565
LAGUNA NIGUEL
CA 92607

PR EXP DATE: 05/16/2013

502 30 0009700 0015 CS 052714 6UVY229 326

EMMANUEL ADETULA
P.O. BOX 1017 Lawndale, CA. 90260
(310) 292-1147 tulatax@gmail.com

July 12, 2013

PROBER & RAPHAEL
A LAW CORP
20750 VENTURA BLVD
WOODLAND HILLS, CA. 91364

CRESCENT BANK & TRUST
P.O. BOX 1097
CHESAPEAKE, VA. 23327

RE: CRECENT BANK & TRUST VS EMMANUEL ADETULA CASE.

Follow up to my letter to you dated October 4, 2012 in response to your debt collect letter dated September 25, 2012. Find attached a final notice to pick up your car from RICK'S AUTOMOTIVE SERVICE AND REPAIR SHOP, If you did not go to the mechanic shop to pick up the car 15 days from today, the car will be given away to be permanently wrecked or dismantled with no cost, you have two options, pick your car or go and pay the mechanic as per invoice attached to help you repair the car and drive away your car, as I said in my letter to you a year ago, you are not going to get any money from me because it was NATIONWIDE and COGENT that breach contract and breach agreement in this case not me, and now they are nowhere to be found, so come take your car instead of asking me for money AFTER 7 years that NATIONWIDE AND COGENT has breach the terms of the agreement and moved out of Los Angeles County.

Thanks

Emmanuel Adetula

UNITED STATES POSTAL SERVICE. Certificate Of Mailing

From: Emmanuel Adetula
P-O BOX 1017
Lawndale CA 90260

To: Prober & Raphael
20750 Ventura Blvd
Woodland Hills CA 913[illegible]

PS Form 3817, April 2007 PSN 7530-02-000-9065

LONG BEACH, CA 90807 JUL 12, 13 AMOUNT $1.20 00088719-04

NOTICE OF STORED VEHICLE (22852 CVC)

NOTE: CHP 180 IS FURNISHED TO ALL PEACE OFFICERS BY THE CALIFORNIA HIGHWAY PATROL

REPORTING DEPARTMENT	LOCATION CODE	DATE / TIME OF REPORT	NOTICE OF STORED VEHICLE DELIVERED PERSONALLY	FILE NO.
SHPD		5-12-14 / 2208		14 - 1205

LOCATION TOWED / STOLEN FROM	ODOMETER READING	VIN CLEAR IN SVS? YES / NO; LIC. CLEAR IN SVS? YES / NO	DATE / TIME DISPATCH NOTIFIED	LOG NO.
ORANGE /	178534			

YEAR	MAKE	MODEL	BODY TYPE	COLOR	LICENSE NO.	ONE / TWO	MONTH / YEAR	STATE
	FORD	FOCUS	SW	BLU		TWO	5-13	CA

VEHICLE IDENTIFICATION NO. — ENGINE NO. — VALUATION BY: OFFICER / OWNER; 0-300 / 301-4000 / 4001+ / $

REGISTERED OWNER: CHRIST CHANNEL CON, 14717 HAWTHORNE BLVD, LAWNDALE CA — SAME AS R/O — LEGAL OWNER

STORED — IMPOUNDED — RELEASED — RECOVERED - VEHICLE / COMPONENT

TOWING / STORAGE CONCERN *(NAME, ADDRESS, PHONE)* — STORAGE AUTHORITY / REASON

TOWED TO / STORED AT — AIRBAG? YES / NO / 1 / 2 — DRIVEABLE? YES / NO / JUNK / UNK — VIN SWITCHED? YES / NO

CONDITION	YES	NO	ITEMS	YES	NO	ITEMS	YES	NO	ITEMS	YES	NO	TIRES / WHEELS	CONDITION
WRECKED			SEAT (FRONT)			REGISTRATION			CAMPER			LEFT FRONT	
BURNED HULK per 431(c) CVC			SEAT (REAR)			ALT. / GENERATOR			VESSEL AS LOAD			RIGHT FRONT	
VANDALIZED			RADIO			BATTERY			FIREARMS			LEFT REAR	
ENG. / TRANS. STRIP			TAPE DECK			DIFFERENTIAL			OTHER			RIGHT REAR	
MISC. PARTS STRIP			TAPES			TRANSMISSION						SPARE	
BODY METAL STRIP			OTHER RADIO			AUTOMATIC						HUB CAPS	
SURGICAL STRIP per 431(b) CVC			IGNITION KEY			MANUAL						SPECIAL WHEELS	

RELEASE VEHICLE TO: R/O OR AGENT — AGENCY HOLD — 22850.3 CVC — GARAGE PRINCIPAL / AGENT STORING VEHICLE *(SIGNATURE)* — DATE / TIME

NAME OF PERSON / AGENCY AUTHORIZING RELEASE — I.D. NO. — DATE — CERTIFICATION: I, THE UNDERSIGNED, DO HEREBY CERTIFY THAT I AM LEGALLY AUTHORIZED AND ENTITLED TO TAKE POSSESSION OF THE ABOVE DESCRIBED VEHICLE

SIGNATURE OF PERSON AUTHORIZING RELEASE — SIGNATURE OF PERSON TAKING POSSESSION

SEE REVERSE FOR INFORMATION

This Vehicle was donated by the Defendant to a Nonprofit agency as Junk, the nonprofit organization could not change the name from the Defendant name at DMV because Cogent Bank is nowhere to be found for the release of liability on DMV records, while Crescent Bank and its Attorney have no right to the release of liability since they lie that Cogent Bank and Nationwide Auction sold them the auto loan, documents and letters on page 74 to page 80 of this book. On May 12, 2014 a staff of Christ Channel who received the donation of this car was driving the car, the police impounded the car. it will cost the Defendant $197 to pay up back DMV fee, $140 to get release approval from the Police and $1,600 to get the vehicle release by the Police garage towing storage as per the letter from the Police Department on page 81.

Emmanuel Adetula
14717 Hawthorne Blvd. Suite B
Lawndale, CA. 90260

October 4, 2012
PROPER & RAPHEL – A LAW CORP
20750 VENTURA BLVD SUITE 100
WOODLAND HILLS, CA. 91364

Re: Account No. 100352739 - PR No. C 184-196

Follow-up to your letter dated September 25, 2012 referenced above, I have no Security and Contract Agreement with CRESCENT BANK & TRUST, I made an arrangement for auto loan with NATIONWIDE AUTION SYSTEMS with their auto financing company COGENT FINANCIAL in 2008, the auction company agreed with me to bring the vehicle back in 2009 for a new Car replacement and for a lower interest because the reason I financed the car was to build my credit rating, but after I paid for one year, I took the car back as agreed , but NATIONWIDE AUCTION has closed shop, moved out of town, and when the used car transmission prevented me to continue the use of the car, then I took the Car to Galpin Ford Auto Dealer for refinancing of a new Car, only to realized that CRESCENT BANK & TRUST who has been collecting the monthly car note on behalf of NATIONWIDE AUCTION and COGENT BANK for 2 years did not even bother report the payment to the credit bureau as required to build my credit, a situation to defeated the only reason why I took a car loan and refinanced the car in the first instance, when I complained to CRESCENT BANK AND TRUST to come and take the Car back since it has a transmission fault and since they are still charging me 29% on top of loan , and since the NATIONWIDE who agreed to take it from me in 2009 has gone out of business, the next thing for Crescent is to refer it to collection and now reported negative nonpayment to the 3 credit bureau to ruin my credit , when I was paying, Crescent did not report my payment, when I complained they should come and reposed the car, they reported the negative nonpayment and contacted you an Attorney to be harassing me for debt collection, while they refused to come for the car. I do not need this car, I already have another car, I do not want to be paying for this car that it's not operational again, I did not intend to keep it after 2009 as agreed with NATIONWIDE , so Please come get the Car instead of asking me to pay you the balance of the car, the only way that I would have pay for this car balance payment would have been if CRESCENT BANK has reported it to the credit bureau in 2008 to 2010, Galpin Ford would have refinanced it, take it from me, and pay for the balance of the car direct to Crescent when I went to buy a new car in 2010, since I have to begin again to refinanced another car again, started again in 2010 as first time car buyer in 2010 despite the fact that I have paid for 2 years earlier without any benefits at 29% interest rate , then started again in 2010 with 29% because CRESCENT did not report the payment to increase my credit score, and give me the opportunity to refinanced it and pay off the car, now that I have another car, and I am no longer using this FORD 2002 Focus, Please tell your client CRESCENT to come and pick it up, because you will not get any money from me for this car , my agreement with NATIONWIDE and Cogent Financial was to take it for one year and use the one year payment to build my credit and bring it back in 2009 to qualify for a new car with a better credit and lower interest rate, it was NATIONWIDE and COGENT that breach contract and breach agreement in this case not me, and now they are nowhere to be found, so come take your car instead of asking me for money AFTER 5 years that NATIONWIDE AND COGENT has breach the terms of the agreement and moved out of Los Angeles County.

Thanks for your understanding.

Emmanuel Adetula

DMV
A Public Service Agency

VEHICLE MOVING PERMIT
(Sections 4002, 4604, 11716 V.C.)

VEHICLE MUST HAVE A VALID PLANNED NON-OPERATION STATUS ON RECORD, BE EXEMPT FROM THE PLANNED NON-OPERATION LAW, OR HAVE REGISTRATION FEES ON DEPOSIT.

VEHICLE LICENSE NUMBER (IF ANY)

VEHICLE IDENTIFICATION NUMBER (VIN): 1FMPU18L9XLC29160
MAKE OF VEHICLE: Ford

The above vehicle will be moved *(check one item only)*:

- ☐ From dealer's, distributor's, or manufacturer's place of business for alteration.
- ☐ From current storage to a new storage location.
- ☐ For repair or alteration.
- ☑ To be permanently wrecked or dismantled.
- ☐ For inspection, smog inspection, or weighing.
- ☐ For construction (incomplete vehicle).
- ☐ From vessel, railroad depot or warehouse to a manufacturer's, re-manufacturer's, distributor's, transporter's, or dealer's warehouse or salesroom.

This permit must be carried with the vehicle when it is moved and presented to the department when the vehicle is registered. This permit is issued for ONE DAY ONLY.

NOTE: This permit does not exempt you from applicable liability insurance laws.

SIGNATURE OF APPLICANT: X
DAYTIME TELEPHONE NUMBER: 310-292-1147

PRINTED NAME OF APPLICANT OR BUSINESS: Adetula Oluwole

ADDRESS: 14717 Hawthorne Blvd #B
CITY: Lawndale

VALID ONLY FOR MOVEMENT ON THIS DATE:

APPROVED BY (Authorized Employee Department of Motor Vehicles or California Highway Patrol)

OFFICE: 1102 FEB 11 2013 X 6
DATE ISSUED

REG 172 (REV 9/99)

Same week of receiving a letter from Los Angeles County Recorder`s office about lien notice, continual reports of negative credit reports to credit bureaus is going on alongside damaging public records as judgment debtor which emanated from a fraudulent used auto car sales in 2008 by an auction company who went into bankruptcy, but an Attorney stole the paperwork and he is using the paperwork to make his law firm rich at the expense of poor American Citizens and this dirty legal job is supported by the government of Los Angeles County judicial process between 2008-2014 and the Attorneys and the Judges are dancing together to perpetuate this Crescent Bank & Trust corporate Crime against Individuals in America.

DEAN C. LOGAN
REGISTRAR-RECORDER/COUNTY CLERK

COUNTY OF LOS ANGELES
REGISTRAR-RECORDER/COUNTY CLERK
P.O. BOX 1250, NORWALK, CALIFORNIA 90651-1250 / www.lavote.net

NOTICE OF INVOLUNTARY LIEN

California Government Code Section 27297.5 requires the County Recorder to notify persons against whom an involuntary lien has been recorded.

You are hereby notified that the enclosed document may constitute a lien against your real property.

California law provides that a lien cannot be released without a signed release from the claimant.

You may wish to contact the lien claimant or your attorney regarding this matter. This department has no involvement with the placement of the lien on your property. This is merely a notification, as required by State Law, to assure that you are aware of the lien.

- **PLEASE DO NOT TELEPHONE THE RECORDER'S OFFICE.**
- **WE HAVE NO ADDITIONAL INFORMATION REGARDING THIS MATTER.**
- **CONTACT THE PERSON CLAIMING THIS LIEN AGAINST YOU.**

3

EJ-001

ATTORNEY OR PARTY WITHOUT ATTORNEY (Name, address, State Bar number, and telephone number):
Recording requested by and return to:

Homan Mobasser Bar No. 251426
PROBER & RAPHAEL
20750 VENTURA BLVD., SUITE 100
WOODLAND HILLS, CA 91364
(818) 227-0100

[X] ATTORNEY FOR [X] JUDGMENT CREDITOR [ ] ASSIGNEE OF RECORD

SUPERIOR COURT OF CALIFORNIA, COUNTY OF LOS ANGELES
STREET ADDRESS: 12720 Norwalk Blvd.
MAILING ADDRESS: Norwalk, CA 90650
CITY AND ZIP CODE:
BRANCH NAME: Southeast District

FOR RECORDER'S USE ONLY

PLAINTIFF: CRESCENT BANK & TRUST

DEFENDANT: EMMANUEL ADETULA AKA EMMANUEL ADETULS

CASE NUMBER: 12CT3326

ABSTRACT OF JUDGMENT—CIVIL AND SMALL CLAIMS [ ] Amended

FOR COURT USE ONLY

1. The [X] judgment creditor [ ] assignee of record applies for an abstract of judgment and represents the following:
   a. Judgment debtor's Name and last known address
   * Emmanuel Adetula AKA Emmanuel Adetuls
   P.O. Box 1017
   Lawndale, CA 90260
   b. Driver's license no. [last 4 digits] and state: [X] Unknown
   c. Social security no. [last 4 digits]: 8896 [ ] Unknown
   d. Summons or notice of entry of sister-state judgment was personally served or mailed to (name and address): Emmanuel Adetula AKA Emmanuel Adetuls P.O. Box 1017 Lawndale, CA 90260
2. [ ] Information on additional judgment debtors is shown on page 2.
3. Judgment creditor (name and address):
   Crescent Bank & Trust
   c/o Prober & Raphael
   20750 Ventura Blvd., # 100, Woodland Hills, CA 91364
4. [ ] Information on additional judgment creditors is shown on page 2.
5. [ ] Original abstract recorded in this county:
   a. Date:
   b. Instrument No.:

Date: March 6, 2014

HOMAN MOBASSER
(TYPE OR PRINT NAME) (SIGNATURE OF APPLICANT OR ATTORNEY)

6. Total amount of judgment as entered or last renewed: $ 9,579.45
7. All judgment creditors and debtors are listed on this abstract.
8. a. Judgment entered on (date): February 14, 2014
   b. Renewal entered on (date):
9. [ ] This judgment is an installment judgment.
10. [ ] An [ ] execution lien [ ] attachment lien is endorsed on the judgment as follows:
    a. Amount: $
    b. In favor of (name and address):
11. A stay of enforcement has
    a. [X] not been ordered by the court.
    b. [ ] been ordered by the court effective until (date):
12. a. [X] I certify that this is a true and correct abstract of the judgment entered in this action.
    b. [ ] A certified copy of the judgment is attached.

[SEAL]

SHERRI R. CARTER

This abstract issued on (date): MAY 0 6 2014

Clerk, by R.S. Wong, Deputy

Form Adopted for Mandatory Use
Judicial Council of California
EJ-001 [Rev. January 1, 2006]

ABSTRACT OF JUDGMENT—CIVIL AND SMALL CLAIMS

C.184-196
Los Angeles

Page 1 of 2
Code of Civil Procedure, §§ 488.480, 674, 700.190

American LegalNet, Inc.
www.FormsWorkflow.com

MICHAEL S. LANGSTON
Chief of Police

POLICE DEPARTMENT

2745 Walnut Avenue • Signal Hill, California 90755 • (562) 989-7200 • FAX (562) 989-7293

May 13, 2014

Christ Channel
14717 Hawthorne Blvd.
Lawndale, CA 90260

Re: Case No. 14-1205

Dear Ms. Channel:

This is to advise you that a vehicle registered to you was impounded by the Signal Hill Police Department on **May 12, 2014**, because the driver either has a suspended driver's license or never had one issued.

Under California law, the impounded vehicle will be held for a **thirty (30) day period**. The owner of the vehicle is responsible for all towing and storage fees. In addition, a $140.00 administrative fee (cash only, exact change) will be required before a release authorization form is issued by the police department.

The California Vehicle Code provides the registered/legal owner of an impounded or stored vehicle the right to a hearing to determine the validity of the impound/storage. Hearings are held at the Signal Hill Police Department on Tuesdays and Thursdays, from 10:00 a.m. to 11:30 a.m. No appointment is necessary. A hearing must be requested within 10 days of the date of this notice.

The vehicle impounded (**2002 Ford Focus, license #6UVY229**) in this case will be available for release from the tow yard on or after **Tuesday, June 10, 2014**. Your vehicle is stored at **Mr. C's Towing, (562) 594-9521**. You may obtain a release form from the Signal Hill Police Department on **Tuesday, June 10, 2014**, from 7:30 a.m. - 5:30 p.m., or thereafter Monday through Thursday from 7:30 a.m. - 5:30 p.m., or Friday from 7:30 a.m. to 4:30 p.m., excluding holidays.

If you have questions about the impounded vehicle, you can contact the Signal Hill Police Department by calling **(562) 989-7200**. A staff member will assist you with the correct information in obtaining your release form.

Sincerely,

Tom Neinast /pp

Tom Neinast
Records Supervisor

"Committed to Excellence in Service"

DMV
A Public Service Agency

VEHICLE MOVING PERMIT
(Sections 4002, 4604, 11716 V.C.)

VEHICLE MUST HAVE A VALID PLANNED NON-OPERATION STATUS ON RECORD, BE EXEMPT FROM THE PLANNED NON-OPERATION LAW, OR HAVE CURRENT REGISTRATION FEES ON DEPOSIT. ALL VEHICLE INFORMATION MUST BE COMPLETED.

VEHICLE LICENSE NUMBER (IF ANY)	MAKE OF VEHICLE	MODEL
6UVY229	FORD	SW
VEHICLE IDENTIFICATION NUMBER (VIN) - IF NONE, WRITE "NONE"		YEAR
1FAHP56372W239326		2002

This permit must be carried with the vehicle when it is moved and submitted to the department when the vehicle is registered. This permit does not exempt you from applicable liability insurance laws.

The above vehicle will be moved *(check one item only)*:

- [ ] For certification (i.e., smog, weight, brake and light, etc.).
- [x] From current storage to a new storage location.
- [ ] For repair or alteration.
- [ ] To be permanently wrecked or dismantled.
- [ ] For VIN assignment.
- [ ] For construction (incomplete vehicle).
- [ ] From dealer's, distributor's, or manufacturer's place of business for alteration.
- [ ] From vessel, railroad depot or warehouse to a manufacturer's, re-manufacturer's, distributor's, transporter's, or dealer's warehouse or salesroom.

Applicant or DMV/CHP agent must enter date prior to movement. This permit is valid for one date only. Any illegible or altered date invalidates permit. Failure to follow these instructions may result in additional fees/penalties and/or citation and possible vehicle impoundment by law enforcement.

THE DATE ENTERED MUST BE WITHIN 60 DAYS FROM THE DATE ISSUED.

VALID ONLY FOR MOVEMENT ON THIS DATE: ____________ (ENTER DATE IN INK)

SIGNATURE OF APPLICANT: X   DAYTIME TELEPHONE NUMBER: (   )

PRINTED NAME OF APPLICANT OR BUSINESS: ADETULS EMMANUEL

ADDRESS / CITY / STATE / ZIP CODE: 14717 HAWTHORNE BLVD #B LAWNDALE CA.

APPROVED BY (AUTHORIZED DMV OR CHP AGENT): X [signature]   DATE ISSUED: 502 MAY 27 2014 3 0

OFFICE: DEPT. OF MOTOR VEHICLES 3615 S HOPE ST. LOS ANGELES CA 90007

REG 172 (REV. 9/2011)

From Storage to Storage since 2009, Crescent Bank and Trust refused to come and pick up its car, if truly this bank purchased the loan from Cogent Bank who entered into contract with Emmanuel Adetuls in 2008. This Trickster Attorney went to court and gets a judgment, filed the judgment debt with Attorney fees with Los Angeles County

Recorder office to put a lien on Emmanuel Adetula home, Crescent Bank debt recovery law firm does not want the car back? but want my home Do you want to get my house for your junk car? This is stealing by legal trick that is encourage by the dancing between the Judge and the Attorney in Los Angeles County under the cover of law is law and this is how the court system works? . This case is not a matter between Crescent Bank and Emmanuel Adetula, this is a case of a Jewish Lawyer enriching himself through legal trick against white and black Gentiles and want to do this same thing to a bad negro boy from Africa. The law is made by man for man, not man for the law. I came here to America by Airplane not by boat. Your father did not transport me here to America by boat to work in your economic field and you get what I work for in America by your own legal trick woven around the perimeter of racism, taking advantage of minorities and poor Americans because you go to law school? and have mastered how to put false legal paperwork together using corporate crime to enrich your law firm? I came to this land to play the game of life on the same level playing ground with any other professionals and this judgment on case number 12CT3326 as decided by the court to-date is not acceptable to me and I reject it. I will not accept a second class citizenship status here before you , just because you study law? , and you know if this is based on simple commonsense you have none to stand before me in this matter. You are a joke, Lawyer boy! Come get your junk car with the original title in your name, and a proof that you have a title on your name at DMV before you filed this case number 12CT3326 in court as the Plaintiff. I have both verbal and written agreement with COGENT FINANCIAL GROUP and NATIONWIDE AUCTION SYSTEM in 2008 not with CRESCENT BANK & TRUST, all documents presented to court by Crescent Bank is a bunch of fabrication of lies and distortion of facts as evidenced in DMV records as of today May 27, 2014.

www.ingramcontent.com/pod-product-compliance
Lightning Source LLC
Chambersburg PA
CBHW070714180526
45167CB00011B/1026

* 9 7 8 1 4 9 9 7 1 5 4 4 6 *